Problem Simplification

Breaking It Down & Working It Out

by

Steven L. Van Dyke

Copyright © 2019 Steven L. Van Dyke, All rights reserved

No part of this publication may be reproduced, distributed, or transmitted in any form or by any means, including photocopying, recording, or other electronic or mechanical methods, or by any information storage and retrieval system without the prior written permission of the publisher, except in the case of very brief quotations in reviews and certain other non-commercial uses permitted by copyright law.

Table Of Contents

Foreword: 5
Chapter 1 — Problem Simplification 7
Chapter 2 — If It's Not Broken, It's Usually Easy To Fix 15
Chapter 3 — Break It Down 25
Chapter 4 — Simple Answers 33
Chapter 5 — Follow The Money 41
Chapter 6 — Adding A Basement 49
Chapter 7 — The 80/20 Rule 57
Chapter 8 — Ideal Gasses 65
Chapter 9 — Calling For Help 73
Chapter 10 — The Real World 81
About the Author 89

Foreword:

The greatest minds in history all have one thing in common: they all took problems that were too complex to solve and found ways to simplify them so they **could** be solved.

Look at Einstein – his Theory of Relativity covers concepts so difficult that at the time there were only a handful of people in the world who could understand them. But unlike some of the others, Einstein kept finding ways to break the problem down into manageable chunks, solving a piece at a time until he had covered everything he could. As an example, one of the problems he simplified away was gravity.

He came up with a simple thought experiment that let him just ignore gravity and the problems it caused. He pointed out that a man in a box could never tell the difference between that box sitting on the ground, and it being an elevator accelerating at a constant rate. From the outside, they're very different, but for the man in the box there's no detectable difference.

Very few of us spend much time trying to advance the basic principles of Physics, but all of us **do** face problems we have to solve. A lot of these problems are so simple we don't even think about them. If we want to get to our office on the fifth floor, we just take the elevator. Sometimes the problems are a little more complex – imagine that the elevator is out of order. In that case, we'd probably just take the stairs. What if the elevator is working, but the lobby is extremely crowded and we're late for a meeting? We can't get to the elevator and it would take too long to take the stairs. My simple solution – I take the stairs up one floor and get on the elevator when someone else gets off.

Probably the number one thing I learned in over 30 years as a professional programmer is that computers **can't** solve complex problems. That's why we need programmers. A programmer's job is to break the complex problem down into simple enough parts for the computer. We can get away with this because the computers can solve a whole slew of simple problems fast enough to make it **look** like they're doing something complicated.

Chapter 1 — Problem Simplification

The purpose of this book is to help you learn how to simplify problems so you can do more with less effort. It will also help you do things you thought you couldn't do at all.

There's no big magic in this book, no special secret knowledge I can impart to you, just a different way of looking at things. I tried to come up with some big, complicated ritual for you to follow, but I wound up simplifying it away. I **did** come up with a "Seven Principles of Problem Simplification," but then I went through the list and simplified it to just three.

For those who want the absolute simplest version, the whole book can be summed up right here in these three principles:

The Three Principles of Problem Simplification

1) Before you try to solve a problem, make sure you know what the problem really is.

2) It's easier to solve a lot of small, simple, problems than one big complex problem.

3) For every problem, there's a clear and simple answer. It's wrong, but figuring out why it's wrong will usually lead to the right answer.

That's it. If you're just browsing this book in the bookstore, you can read through the list a couple more times and be done. The rest of this book is simply an explanation of those principles, how I arrived at them, and even relating some of the ones that I simplified out of the original list.

And, of course, you can't have a book like this without a mnenomic to help you remember the main points, as one of my beta readers pointed out. We couldn't come up with one with the Principles in the right order. Best we could do was PIE. Really, once you start thinking about pie it's hard not to (sorry if I made you hungry).

P – Pieces. Cut your problem up into easier to solve pieces just like you would cut up a pie.
I – Identify. Before you try to solve your problem, make sure you know what the problem really is.
E – Easy Answer.   Yes, that simple answer is probably wrong, but it will help you find the real one.

I'll try to follow a similar format in each chapter, in case you're in a hurry or want to keep the book around for a while as a reference. It's also handy if you want to show a particular part to someone else.

For the rest of this chapter let me tell you some of how I came to learn about problem simplification and some of what it's meant to me. Because I've been a computer programmer for so long, I talk about computers a lot, but don't worry — you shouldn't have to know anything about computers to understand what I'm saying.

Many years ago, way back before the IBM PC, I got myself a personal computer. I was in college and had started taking programming courses, so I had a justification, but I really got it just because it was neat. It was a Radio Shack TRS-80, Model 1, Level II (yes, I'm old). It was pretty advanced for the time and even had its own built-in BASIC to make it easy to program. Well, I decided that I wanted to learn Assembly language, even though programming in Assembler was supposed to be difficult. When I got to looking at it though, it turned out that Assembly language **itself** was really pretty simple. There aren't that many instructions and none of them really do very much. Which is what people really meant when they said Assembler was difficult: the **language** is simple, but **using** it is difficult because you have to break things down into such tiny pieces. It's like building a sand castle one grain at a time. You can do some **amazing** things, but it can get **really** tedious.

The things I learned writing Assembly language have served me well over the years, and I've always felt it made me a better programmer. If you're into computers, I encourage you to learn Assembler and to try your hand at writing a few non-trivial programs.

One example of how learning Assembly language helped me learn problem simplification is the way multiplication is performed in Assembler. On most modern microprocessors there is an instruction that does multiplication, but even on those you sometimes need to know how to do it "raw." The trick that you use is to break the multiplication down into its basic actions — a series of additions. Remember when you learned how to multiply? You learned to multiply the top number by each digit in the bottom number and add the partial products together. Well, in the binary math computers use, you do the same thing but you don't have to know as large a 'times' table. Instead of having to know 0x0 through 9x9, you only have to know 0x0 to 1x1. If you're multiplying by a 0, the answer is 0. If you've got a 1, the answer is the number you're multiplying. In other words, you either add or you don't — how much simpler can you get? Actually, I'm simplifying some of the issues involved, partly because this isn't a book about computer programming but mostly because this **is** a book about simplification.

Getting away from computers for a moment, another example of problem simplification that I ran across was presented as an example of alternate thinking. The example was a group trying to remove a gear that was rusted on to an axle. After everyone had been trying various methods of pulling the axle free, another person simply braced the gear and gave the axle a good solid whack with a sledge hammer, shooting it across the room. Getting the gear off the axle was too difficult a problem to solve. By changing the problem to getting the gear and axle apart, he was able to find a solution to the simpler problem of getting the axle out of the gear.

It's examples like these that led me to my first principle of problem simplification — making sure you know what the problem is before you try to solve it. The next time you're faced with a problem, take a moment and see if you can turn it around. Write down a list of all the different ways to state the problem and the most obvious solution for each one. You'll often find an easier way to solve your problem. Sometimes you find out you were working on the wrong problem to begin with.

One advantage I've always had in problem solving is that I have a knack for finding simple answers to complex questions. The simple answer usually **isn't** right, but in working out **why** it isn't right, you can generally find the answer that **is** right.

One of the places I worked produced biomedical equipment, mostly devices for respiratory monitoring. We even had our own in-house physicist who helped us design new devices. For one project, he wanted to have two perfectly matched infra-red sources so he could see how much of the signal was absorbed by the sample gas. The problem was that there wasn't really room in the box for two sources — in fact, he was having trouble getting things arranged even with **one** source. Plus, since the sources needed to be so closely matched, the unit was looking like it would be too expensive to build. When he explained the problem to me, I immediately knew the simple answer. What he needed was a way to use one source, split the light, and be able to pipe it around. Fiber optic light pipes for infra-red were too expensive, and it would have been too hard to split the beam, but my suggestion got around all of that. My suggestion was: shiny pipe. Take a 'Y' shaped piece of pipe, chrome the **inside**, and use it as a light pipe. The physicist started to explain why that wouldn't work, but by the time he got half-way through, he was figuring out ways to **make** it work. It took him a month or so of research, but he got the unit working just the way he wanted, and in the end his two word explanation of the secret was: shiny pipe.

This is why my third principle is:

"Every problem has a clear, simple answer. It's wrong, but figuring out why it's wrong will usually lead you to the right answer."

So as you read through this book, if you think I'm wrong, take the time to figure out **why** I'm wrong and you just might come up with the right answer yourself. Which would mean this book was worth reading anyway, wouldn't it?

Chapter 2 — If It's Not Broken, It's Usually Easy To Fix

"Before you try to solve a problem, make sure you know what the problem really is."

There's a reason I made that my first principle.

If you think about it, the ultimate simple solution to a problem is not having to solve it at all. If you can figure that out **before** you spend a lot of time and effort trying to 'solve' something that's not really a problem to begin with, you can save yourself a lot of pain.

If you think it's painful finding out that all of the work you've been doing is a waste; add in that you **still** have to solve the real problem, once you figure out what it is.

Plus, it's really hard to solve a vague problem. The tighter, more specific the problem's description is, the easier it is to solve. The bigger and broader the problem, the less likely it is to **ever** get solved.

How can you tell if you're looking at the real problem?

In some ways you can look at the length of the problem description to see how well it's defined. **Usually**, the shorter the description, the less well defined the problem is. Sometimes you have a problem that's so clear you don't need a long winded explanation. When something rips the roof off of your house "The roof's gone" seems to cover things pretty well to me. Mostly though, you want to watch out for those short problem statements. Here's a list of well-defined problems that should be easy to solve:

1) The battery is dead in my watch.
2) The airline sent my luggage to Buffalo and me to LA so I have no clean underwear.
3) I can't remember the name of the person to whom I was just introduced.

Now here's a list of some poorly defined problems that are probably impossible to solve:

1) The economy
2) Campaign financing
3) Sales are down 20%

And just to be fair, here are a couple of problems that are pretty well defined, but look pretty tough to solve.

1) The boss of the customer to whom you're making the big sales pitch is someone you cheated back when **they** were working for **you**.
2) In the new hardware you've just started shipping, the battery doesn't last long enough to be useful. There's no room to put a bigger one in the case without redesigning the unit. For even more fun, the only type of battery

that gives more life in the same size has a nasty tendency of catching on fire and/or exploding.

Going back to the set of ill-defined problems, let's look at the one we **might** be able to solve, if we just work on it a while. Rather than campaign financing, we will tackle the less ambitious "sales are down 20%" one.

The reason we probably can't solve this problem is that we don't know **why** sales are down. The real problem, whatever it is that's causing this slump, may or may not be something over which we have any control. We're going to have to figure out how to find the real problem before we can solve it.

One of the ways to try to find the real problem is to write it down in different ways, along with possible reasons. I call this the **because** game. For this example, I would try to write all of the variations I could find of "Sales are down 20% **because...**"

If we try that, we might wind up with something like this:

Sales are down 20%.

Sales are down 20% **because** we're not closing enough deals.

Sales are down 20% **because** our customers never call us.

Sales are down 20% **because** our repeat customers stopped calling us.

I'm beginning to see a pattern here, which is good since I'm trying to show one. Notice that it seems like our sales problem revolves around calls. We don't seem to be getting as many calls as we used to, so it's harder for our sales force to close deals.

So now we can start over with "We're not getting as many calls because…"

What changed since last quarter, or whenever it was that we're comparing against? Make a list of everything you can think of that's changed and try each one as a 'because'.

We'll say that we're looking at last quarter and since then:

1) We've hired a new sales associate named Joe.
2) We've changed our pricing breaks.
3) We got a new phone system.
4) Our biggest competitor announced a major promotion.

Trying these out we get:

1) Sales are down 20% **because** we're not getting as many calls **because** of the new guy, Joe.

2) Sales are down 20% **because** we're not getting as many calls **because** we changed our pricing breaks.

3) Sales are down 20% **because** we're not getting as many calls **because** of our new phone system.

4) Sales are down 20% **because** we're not getting as many calls **because** of our competitor's big sale.

Now we're getting somewhere. Each of these is something we can check.

We can check Joe's figures against the rest of the team to see if he's pulling sales down.

We can look at the orders we **are** getting and how they relate to our new pricing structure and compare that against the orders we got last quarter.

We can spend some time calling our own phone system from the outside, to get a customer's perspective.

We can ask our customers what they think about the new phone system.

We can try to see if our competition's numbers are up enough to account for our loss.

When we look into these things we may find out that Joe's not doing quite as well as the more experienced guys. He's doing a pretty good job, though, and besides, the other salespeople's figures are down too.

Checking the pricing structure hopefully shows that the orders we're getting now tend to be just a bit bigger than they were before, but we might see that we're not getting as many small orders.

Calling in to check on our new phone system we find that now **every** call is answered right away, and the new voice-mail system allows you direct access to the person you called. If they're not there, the system even lets you leave a detailed message directly with them instead of just giving a secretary your name and number.

As far as we can tell, the competition's sale **is** pulling in more business for them, but they only seem to be up by about 5% of the sales we're missing.

The only change we're seeing that we **can't** account for the effects of is the new phone system. It could be that after we talk to our customers about it, we find out that the real problem is that sales are down 20% because our customers don't like our new voice mail system. **Now** we have a problem we can solve.

If instead of doing all of this, we just decided that sales were down because of Joe and fired him, we might wind up like this:

The rest of the sales team now has to deal with the customers Joe had, **plus** find and train a replacement. The extra workload makes it even harder for clients to get through to them on the phone, dumping more of them into our voice mail from hell. Tired of never getting to talk to a real person, and seeing our competitor's ads, more and more of our customers turn to them. Seeing their business go up while ours goes down, we decide to have a big sale. More people try to call, more folks wind up in voice mail, etc.

We're in a downward spiral, and if we don't find the real problem in time, we'll just keep wasting resources on solving the wrong problem until the wasted effort drags us down to our doom.

Another danger of trying to solve the wrong problem is the risk of breaking something that works. In the case we just looked at, Joe was a good and useful part of the sales team. Firing him was not only wasted effort (since it didn't do anything to fix the phone system) it actually made things worse by sending more people to it.

As a programmer, I could tell you a **lot** of stories of putting in some code to fix one problem and causing a slew of others. Usually we catch these things in our own testing. If there's a Quality Assurance department, they generally catch them in their testing. But anyone who's ever bought a software upgrade knows that some of them slip through.

The more precisely you define your problem, the more likely you are to be able to test it. In our example, when we checked each of our four possible problems, we **thought** it might be the phone system. Remember though that I said "after we talk to our customers about it." If we hadn't done that extra research we wouldn't have **known** that the problem was our snazzy new voice mail system.

And what if the problem **wasn't** the phone system, but our new price breaks? If we just looked at what changed and said, "Well, we did new price breaks, but those were based on what our customers want. That new phone system they sold us must be the problem." We'd probably start tearing it up, inconveniencing everybody that calls and probably losing sales.

But, suppose that in this case the real problem is that our new pricing structure is costing us most of our small orders and they made up more of our business than we thought. Now we're still not getting the small orders. Not only that, our big order customers **liked** our new phone system and thought it made us look more professional. Now they're upset about the phone problems caused by ripping out the voice mail so they're calling our competitors. If losing our small orders cost us 20%, what will losing a couple of our biggest accounts do?

When you think about what can happen when you don't work on solving the right problem, it's enough to make you afraid to do anything. Trust me, that can be bad too.

There are times, though, when you only **think** you have a problem. In those cases, the time and energy you spend trying to solve the non-problem is completely wasted **plus** you run the risk of breaking something.

Let's look at our test case once again. Only this time, instead of starting from "sales are down 20%" let's start with "small orders are down 35%." We know what we're doing, so we fiddle with the price breaks, move some people around, mess with the phone system, everything we can think of to change. In this case, though, the problem is that our small orders were only down because our new price breaks encouraged more people to make larger orders. Overall sales aren't actually down, they're **up**, or at least they **were** until we started messing with things.

So remember,

"Before you try to solve a problem, make sure you know what the problem really is."

- A good way to make sure you know what the problem is to try and restate it. The more ways you can restate the problem, the less likely it is to be well defined. When you know **exactly** what's wrong, you'll be able to give less precise descriptions of the problem, but not **different** ones.

- If you're still looking for the problem, or think you might be, play the 'because' game.

- **Always** look for ways to turn the problem around, even if you have a good idea of what it may be, and a clear path to solving it. Looking at the problem from another angle will often reveal other problems the first one was hiding. You'll usually wind up having to solve those previously hidden problems eventually anyway, and sometimes solving one of these hidden problems will make the obvious problem go away. If your deliveries are always late because your truck is in bad shape, maybe it's just that you have a major pothole in your driveway.

Chapter 3 — Break It Down

"It's easier to solve a lot of small, simple, problems than one big complex problem."

When you state it flat out like that, it seems rather obvious. It's like saying "falling in water can get you wet."

But it also underscores the importance of planning, and one of the most fundamental aspects of planning — breaking the problem down into manageable chunks.

Remember, the ancient strategy for conquering the world isn't just "Conquer the world," it's "**Divide** and conquer."

Very few recipes tell you to just throw everything in a pot and start boiling. Some do, soups and stews mainly, plus a lot of mixes and packaged meals, but you know what I mean. There's a sequence of actions followed in cooking. It often involves making parts of the recipe as separate items all of their own. When you make a pie, you make (or if you're lazy buy) the crust as a separate item. Sure, it winds up being an integral part of the pie when it's done, but you start with it as its own project.

When you look at a problem, look for ways to break it down into discrete chunks. Not only will that make the problem easier to solve, if you're working as part of a group, it's just about impossible **not** to do it this way, at least if you want to get anything done. The more you can break the project down, the more independently you can work. In the pie example, the person making the crust can be in another state, and do their part weeks before the rest of the 'pie team.' That's pretty much the way it is when you buy a ready-made crust.

The art of computer programming is really the art of breaking problems down into manageable pieces. This is so fundamental that the current standard is called "Object Oriented Design." It's based on breaking the problem down into chunks, called objects, that can be reused later for other projects. There's also a thriving market for what are known as 'object libraries' or collections of ready made pieces.

In other words, if you're doing Object Oriented Programming, when you go to program a 'pie' application, you can either buy a ready made 'crust' object or use one you made earlier. It's just like when you make a real pie, except that you're less likely to want your 'crust' to turn out flaky.

You can use this object oriented approach in solving a lot of your problems. You probably already do, whether you realize it or not. Doing your taxes is an exercise in solving an object oriented problem. Each part of the overall 'problem' of how much money the government gets to take from you is a form. You must assemble the correct set of forms in the proper order to solve the problem. If you get it right, you often get rewarded with the opportunity to write them a check so they can have even more of your hard-earned income. Sigh. Oh well, I never said all problems were **fun** to solve.

I can't seem to get away from these non-fun examples of how you see real-world problems broken down in a systematic and organized way. Another good example is car repair. The service manager will break down your "My car won't start." problem into a whole list of sub-problems and give you estimates for each one. Some parts will be dependent on the results of other parts, and it seems that they usually find a couple of extra things while they're in there. Still, it's pretty much just a process of breaking the problem down into discrete sections. Your "My car won't start." problem that's hard to deal with becomes things like "The battery is old and weak," "Starter solenoid is hanging," and "Out of gas." All small, simple to solve problems.

One interesting aspect of breaking things down is that, some of these sub-problems can be so discrete that it doesn't really matter who does them. If you're just fixing up your car, rather than repairing it, you might go to one place to get it painted and to have a new stereo and a sun-roof installed. However, it's likely that two of the three tasks of your "Fix up the car" problem will be contracted out.

This is the basis of the niche market. There can be a lot

of money made in doing parts of things that are either difficult for people to do themselves or are best done by someone more experienced. Keeping with the car theme, things like boring out cylinders and rebuilding starters provide a good living to a lot of folks.

If you find yourself with a flair for solving some little part of a problem, look at marketing yourself as a specialist in that niche. I don't necessarily mean starting a business and running an ad in the paper. It could be just spreading the word at work that you're willing to help to do the graphics for reports and such. It could even be your family knowing that **you're** the one who can get the dog to take his pill. Doing something well feels good, so if you find something you're good at, try to find a way to do more of it; at least if it's something socially acceptable. If it isn't, contact either the media or the government, and they'll probably have a place for you. Myself, I'm good at solving problems and this book is an extension of that skill.

Niche markets leads me into the custom vs. mass produced arena. Mass produced **anything** always creates some type of niche market. It's true in whatever you buy – cars, software, clothing, houses. A common thread that runs through these niches is that some part of each is devoted to solving a **problem** with the mass produced product. The problems don't even have to be something other people would consider a 'real' problem. A lot of the niche markets for cars are for problems like 'it's not fast enough' or 'it doesn't look fancy enough.'

Having a car that won't bounce several feet into the air is **not** a problem for the average person, but there's a thriving industry in fitting out cars to do just that.

So why do we use mass produced things if they all have so many problems? This actually ties in with my theme for this section: the mass produced whatever solves **most** of the problem. It may not solve it in quite the way I **want** to solve it, but it gets me **closer** to a solution. If I have an odd-shaped document to mail, I **could** make my own envelope. It's a lot more likely, however, that I'll buy whatever one I can find in which it will fit and then either fold my document to fit the envelope, or add padding to make the envelope fit my document. The problem of adapting to a standard solution is a **simpler** problem than creating a custom solution.

Take a look at your problem. Is it a problem that already has a standard solution? If you don't think it is, **why** do you think the problem's unique? It could well be that you're right – there **is** no mass-market, one-size-fits-all solution to your problem. But there may well be something that's **close**. Don't forget to look at other problems **you've** solved in the past. You could well already have a '95%' solution!

Sometimes, it's a lot cheaper to figure out how to solve your problem by using something off-the-shelf than it is to have something custom made. If you're a normal sized person, you can save a lot of money by shopping at K-Mart instead of having a personal tailor. On the other hand, if you've got three arms and a 42-inch neck, it's going to be cheaper for you in the long run to pay the price for a custom fit from the beginning than to spend all the time and effort working with standard stuff that never will come out right.

Solve as many parts of your problem as you can by using things that are already available and effective. Save your extra effort for only those parts that really are unique. When you're breaking down your problem, try to keep a list of 'known solutions' in the back of your mind and break things down to fit them. If you find that makes the solution more trouble than the original problem, just break it down again until you get something that you think will work.

When you break a problem down into parts there may be standard answers for, but you find that there aren't any, you've just found a potential niche market. If enough people have the same problem, and are willing to pay for your solution, you could wind up being ever so glad about the problem you originally set out to solve.

One of the most important parts of figuring out how to solve your problem, is figuring out how to solve it **again**. There are very few problems that only have to be solved once, and even those usually include some sort of maintenance requirement. Make sure you don't replace today's headache with tomorrow's nightmare.

If you've ever worked on your own car, you're sure to have cursed the designers who made a particular part so hard to replace. Designing things so you have to replace an entire tail-light assembly if a bulb blows might make the original manufacturing easier, but it's not going to win you any awards on down the road. And don't get me started on cars where you have to take a wheel off to replace the battery!

One of the **most** important parts of solving the problem 'for all time' is **documenting** how you solved it the first time. I can't tell you how many times I, in my role as a programmer, have cursed the name of the idiot before me (often myself before I wised up) who failed to document what this blasted chunk of code did and **why** it did it that way. If you find out that the copier will keep jamming until you run a paper towel through it to clean out the lint, write that down somewhere and tell a few folks. If you don't, they're going to call you on your vacation and be pretty upset that you can't remember.

So, to summarize; break your problems down into chunks and look at each chunk as a separate problem. The more independent your chunks are, the easier it is to get someone **else** to solve them for you. You might even be able to find a ready made solution.

Chapter 4 — Simple Answers

As I mentioned back in Chapter 1, one of the principles that I chose as key is:

"Every problem has a clear and simple answer. It's wrong, but figuring out why it's wrong will usually lead you to the right answer."

Finding the simple answer is often a case of backing up from your detailed view of the problem to that fuzzier overview – something I'll talk about in Chapter 8. Simple answers are simple in part because they don't deal with the details. Of course, that's usually why they're wrong, but as I said, they **do** give you a starting point for finding the real answer.

Let me use the magic of cut and paste here to go back to Chapter 1 for my story about simple answers:

*One of the places I worked produced biomedical equipment, mostly devices for respiratory monitoring. We even had our own in-house physicist who helped us design new devices. For one project, he wanted to have two perfectly matched infra-red sources so he could see how much of the signal was absorbed by the sample gas. The problem was that there wasn't really room in the box for two sources – in fact, he was having trouble getting things arranged even with **one** source. Plus,* *since the sources needed to be so closely matched, it was looking like it was going to make the unit too expensive to build. When he explained the problem to me, I immediately knew the simple answer. What he needed was a way to use one source, split the light, and be able to pipe it around. Fiber optic light pipes for infra-red were too expensive, and it would have been too hard to split the beam, but my suggestion got around all of that. In two words, my suggestion was: shiny pipe. Take a 'Y' shaped piece of pipe, chrome the **inside**, and use it as a light pipe. Dick, the physicist, started to explain why that wouldn't work, but by the time he got half-way through, he was figuring out ways to **make** it work. It took him a month or so of research, but he got the unit working just the way he wanted, and in the end his two word explanation of the secret was: shiny pipe.*

The reason I'm bringing this up again is to point out something I just touched on at the end of that anecdote: the simple answer for your problem is often a good summary description of the real answer. The pipe that Dick wound up using to turn one IR source under the sample chamber into two matched sources next to the sample chamber was an interesting piece of work. The lining wasn't exactly chrome, as best I can recall, and he had to take some care with the geometry of the pipe, but in talking to, say, the board of directors, he just said it was shiny pipe.

So there's your first clue to finding that simple answer: try to explain your problem, and it's possible solution, to

someone who has no real idea what you're talking about.
Spouses, relatives, children, pets, management, just find
someone uninvolved that you can try to explain things
to. By forcing yourself to explain everything to
someone who not only doesn't know the details, but
doesn't **want** to know the details, you're forced to gloss
over them. That's what gives you that simple answer.

Most of the examples I've been giving have been pretty
thin on details, which has made it easy for me to give
simple, straightforward answers. It's a bit of a setup, but
do you want to wade through 20 pages of minutia about
someone else's situation or do you want to solve your
own problems? Anyway, the key here is to use
explaining your problem as a way of finding the simple
answer. If you're actually working with someone that
can talk back to you, they might just give you your
simple answer, just as I gave Dick what he needed for
his problem. When they make a stupid suggestion, don't
just say it won't work. Take a bit of time to figure out,
and perhaps explain, **why** it won't work.

When you find your simple answer, there's one thing
that it is absolutely **vital** that you remember: **it's wrong**.
It's only the starting point for the real answer; a
summarized description. If you try to use the simple
answer without working out the details, bad things will
happen.

I'm sorry to keep harping on this, but it's amazing how
many people get to the simple answer and never go any

further. They wind up wasting tremendous amounts of time and effort finding out that they didn't actually have a real answer to their problem to begin with.

To be honest, I don't see **people** doing this so much as organizations. It seems that the larger the organization, the more likely they are to flail away trying to use unrefined answers to their problems. I'm sure you've been involved in efforts at work where no one involved had any idea why you were wasting your time on this slow motion train wreck. Everyone knew what you were doing wouldn't work, yet you were helpless to stop the project as it rumbled on its way to oblivion. If you were lucky, the blasted thing managed to die without taking too much else with it. Most of the projects that tail off, slowly grinding down over a long period of time, are attempts to use simple answers to solve complex problems. The programs that shut down in some spectacular fashion, taking people, departments, sometimes whole companies, with them are also often simple answer mania gone wrong. If you've been fortunate enough to avoid any of these demented beasts, just pick almost any long-standing government program.

I think the basic cause of this simple answer tar pit is communication. The more people you have to tell about something, the more likely you are to use the short, simple, version. If the details don't get distributed, then you wind up trying to do the wrong thing. The best analogy I can come up with is the difference between talking to a single person, and passing on the news to a large crowd without any sort of amplification.

That 'large group/frequent repetition' thing is probably why politicians and political programs are so likely to fall into the simple answer trap. The complex social problems that they're trying to deal with are difficult to solve. Even if they have a workable solution, it's probably not something they can explain in one or two soundbytes. Say that the solution to some problem involves tracking down particular offenders based on carefully chosen criteria and locking them up while making sure they stay separated to disrupt their communications. You just **know** that's going to get simplified back down to "Take the criminals off the streets" and they're going to wind up sending jay walkers to Attica, clogging the courts and filling the prisons to the point the people the program was meant to get have to be given early release due to overcrowding. I'm not referring to any particular program, just pointing out how these things happen.

You can run into this same sort of thing in your work as well. After you've gone through all of the work of finding a solution to the crisis of the day, carefully working it out and coming up with a catchy slogan for the coffee mugs, how do you avoid getting it deformed by office politics?

I suppose the only way to avoid these side effects is to do the unnatural thing and shut up. Tell them what your answer is, give them the simplified version when you pitch it, and then **don't do it again**. If you insist on referencing the **real** answer, you might be able to avoid having people fixate on the simple answer. After you get the project going, think carefully before you do any more promotion. Will you be able to tell this person/group the real answer, or will they walk off repeating the stripped down version? The reason this is important is that the information you give is like a stone dropping into your 'resource pool'. It's going to spread out, simplifying as it goes. Past a certain distance, it doesn't really matter **what** you said. The trick is to control the release and distribution of the information so that it doesn't get hopelessly garbled until it's out **past** the circle of people you need to accomplish your objectives. You kind of want that simple, but wrong, answer to be the one that reaches your competition. Let them waste **their** resources, but make sure everyone working on **your** problem really does understand what you're trying to get done. It's like building the pyramids – you've got hundreds of people pulling on ropes to move this giant stone. It really helps if most of them are headed in **one** direction. It's even better if it's the **right** direction.

So for the simple version of this chapter, look for that simple, obvious answer to your problem, but realize that it's probably wrong. If you're having trouble finding that simple answer, explain your problem to others who aren't involved. The simplification you'll need to do to achieve this will tend to drive you toward a simple answer. When you find your simple answer, **don't stop**.

When you share your solution, make sure you get the **real** answer across, not just the simple one. One example of this would be, say, deriving three principles of Problem Simplification, and then writing a book to explain them.

Chapter 5 — Follow The Money

The guiding principle for this chapter is:

"Sometimes it's cheaper to spend money on simplifying a problem than it is to solve the complex version."

Sometimes we'll spend just **massive** amounts of time and energy to solve a problem that we really shouldn't be messing with. Usually this is because we're trying to save money.

In a way, I owe this book to a time I was following company rules about saving money...

In one of the programming jobs I've had over the years, we made our own computers to be used to control equipment. I was working on the software part of a new system, with new and possibly problematic hardware, and something wasn't working right. It didn't **seem** to be the software, but the hardware kept passing various tests. Anyway, a technician and I spent most of a day trying to figure the blasted thing out. Finally, one of the older technicians came over to see what we were doing. We explained the situation to him. He asked a few more questions about what we had done. When he was satisfied that we had done everything reasonable to get the board to work, he told us: "This is obviously a complex and subtle problem. The only thing to do here is to simplify it." Then he picked up a hammer, unplugged the board, and gave it a whack. "There," he said, "now your problem is simple. You need a new board." The new board, of course, worked fine, allowing me to get back to work on the software.

Those boards weren't cheap. He avoided most of the parts we could pull off and reuse, but it was still a couple of hundred dollars. **But** between the other technician and myself, we'd already spent almost that much in what it was costing the company to have us fooling around with that stupid board. We didn't think about getting rid of the board because "it almost worked." If we **had** gotten a new board right away, we would actually have saved the company a fair chunk of change.

As you can tell from this book, that basic advice on simplifying the problem has stuck with me. I can't promise you'll get to smash anything with a hammer after reading this book, but at least you'll have a good excuse if you do.

How many times have you needed something done around the house and decided to do it yourself, to save money? By the time I buy the tools and supplies I need, go back and get new materials to replace the ones I ruined learning to use the tools, and get a couple other things to fix the damage I caused to parts of the house that didn't need fixing before I started, I've generally spent a ton of money just to get things ready to bring in a pro to clean up my mess. That's why now I at least **look** at what a pro would cost **first**. When my roof needed new shingles, I quickly found a company that would do the whole job for less than the estimate the hospital gave me for what I would need if I fell off the roof onto the driveway.

This sort of thing points out one of the most common ways people get trapped into chasing false economy. That "it's cheaper to do it myself" mindset carries over into business as well. Many people, especially in small businesses, resist using consultants because "it's too expensive."

Well now, let's take a look at that, shall we?

First, how much is your time worth? Even assuming that you do the whole thing in time you would have otherwise wasted, take a moment and figure out what you would have charged someone else if you did the same project for them.

Second, if you're doing that (whatever **that** is), who's doing your job? Also, what is it costing your business to have you tied up in this 'other' thing?

Third, how fast do you need it? Even if your business can afford to have **you** tied up for who knows how long, how long can they afford to wait for this project to get done? About the only way you'll get something done as fast as a trained professional is if you **are** a trained professional. Heck, I've been a professional programmer for over thirty years, and there are a lot of things where I'll go straight to someone else. I **know** they have more, or more recent, experience in that particular area that will let them do the job faster and probably better.

Finally, what's the cost of getting it wrong? I don't mean just the fact that you'll have to do everything over, burning up more of your otherwise productive time. I don't even mean the costs of any tools and materials you used in this attempt. I'm talking about the cost of having a bad solution. Whenever there's a change in my tax situation, or if I have **any** doubts about my taxes, I go to a professional. The IRS has spent a lot of time and effort to make us fear the cost of getting our taxes wrong.

For a real world example from my past, one of my co-workers at a former job had been involved in a project where they made a battery operated item. To save power, it turned itself off after you stopped using it. It would also display a warning when the battery got low. Unfortunately, when it was displaying this low battery warning it **didn't** turn itself off. So as soon as your battery got low, it would turn itself on and run the battery flat as fast as possible. They didn't find this error until they got complaints back from customers. They decided it was acceptable (and cheaper) to just send customers who complained coupons for new batteries than to recall all of the units in the field and replace the chip with the defective program. They **did** though, have to budget making a new chip for the next version of the device, and they **did** lose at least a few sales because of this flaw.

When you add all of those factors together, writing your own inventory control system doesn't sound like such a good idea anymore, does it? Like I said, I try to stay away from any home repairs with possible expensive consequences.

Sometimes there are unexpected benefits to spending money on simplifying problems. Back in the old days, the oil companies spent a small, but annoying, amount of money to get rid of the leftover goo after they refined oil. One executive decided he'd had enough and told one of the company's researchers to stop what he was doing and find something to do with 'that stuff'. 'That stuff' became plastic and is now an industry as large as, or possibly even larger, than the oil industry.

Everyone's heard about the spin-offs from the Apollo space program. If it's small and electronic, it can probably be traced back. But the fun thing is that most people don't know the real reason **why**. It wasn't the space program itself, really. After all, the Russians were working just as hard as we were, but they're not really known for their advances in electronics. The actual, honest-to-God reason why we concentrated so much on miniaturization and power savings was because we had wimpy rockets. To this day the Russians still have better rockets. They could **afford** to loft big bulky batteries and clunky equipment. We had to shave off every ounce and cubic inch we could. For us, it was cheaper to make equipment fit the rocket's capabilities than it was to make bigger and better rockets. As we went along, the bigger rockets we made were able to lift proportionally more because we'd already made the stuff they were made with (as well as the stuff they had to carry) smaller and lighter. By 'wasting' money on miniaturization, we wound up getting a lot more bang for our buck. Not to mention camcorders, digital watches, CD players, and cell phones.

I saw a news piece recently about a company that raises worms and sells them for bait. One of their problems was what to do with the **tons** (literally) of worm poop their charges produce each year. Next time you buy a bag of 'worm castings' to fertilize your garden or flower bed, you just might be sending them a little money for their solution.

Simpler problems are not only **easier** to solve, they're usually **cheaper**. The trick is to figure out when spending money on making a problem simpler makes sense. The ideal situation is when you know about how much each of three things is going to cost: A) the cost of solving the complex problem, B) the cost of solving the simple problem, and C) the cost of turning the complex problem into a simple problem. As long as (B + C) is less than A, we should spend the money. The trick to this is figuring it all out **before** we spend any money. I think I'll take a tip from our old school math books here and say; "The solution to this is left as an exercise for the student."

Chapter 6 — Adding A Basement

There's a very simple rule for navigating through space:

"The energy required to change course increases geometrically with time, so make sure you know where you're going before you leave."

Actually, I added the "make sure you know where you're going" part.

What that is saying is that, if you wait twice as long to change course, it's going to take four times the energy. For example, if you figure out at one minute into your trajectory that you're off course and need to burn 3 lbs. of fuel to get back on course, if you wait until minute two, you'll need 6 lbs. At minute 3, 12 lbs., and so on. Basically, try **really** hard to get it right the first time, and check your work as soon as possible.

In my years as a programmer, I always had trouble explaining to people why some of the changes they wanted were done in two days and others I said just couldn't be done, when they couldn't see much difference between them. I finally hit upon comparing the project to constructing a building. Most people don't do enough programming to understand how it works, but we see enough buildings being built that it's fairly easy to understand things in construction terms.

Some changes are just additions — "Add a door over there, and another room on the back." Most of these can be done without any real difficulty. Sometimes you run into the equivalent of putting a door in a load-bearing wall, or wanting two rooms to occupy the same spot, but that just makes things a little more interesting.

Some changes are purely cosmetic — "Paint it blue." These also tend to take just whatever time they take. There's nothing extra you have to do, but you are talking about a different time scale if 'it' is a door than if 'it' is everything in, on, and around the Empire State Building.

But **some** changes just aren't any fun at all. These are the ones I call 'basement' changes because they're the moral equivalent of adding a basement to a building. It's not that hard to do **if** you do it at the right time – while you're working with blueprints, rather than when you're sitting in an office on the 42nd floor. In fact, it's even better to make this sort of change when you don't even have blueprints yet.

These 'basement' changes are like course changes in a project, and as I said above, the longer you wait to change course, the more it's going to cost you.

How much time have you spent with a project that was "almost done?" Quite often, a project that's stuck at 90% is stuck there because someone wants, or needs, one of those basement changes made. If no one realizes, or wants to admit, that the only way to accomplish this is to go back to the drawing board, you can spend a **long** time, and a **lot** of money, trying to get the project finished.

If you're having problems getting a project finished, and find yourself seemingly glued to that '90% done' status, take a good long look at the changes you're still trying to get working. What level do these changes need to be made at? Are you adding a door, adding a room, painting it blue, or are you trying to add a basement? If you're stuck at that 'almost done' state, you generally have one of two things going on (you only get both on those 'special' projects). Either you're A) chasing a moving target, or B) adding a basement.

In some ways, the answer to both of these situations is the same: somebody is going to have to make a decision and stick to it. If you're chasing a moving target, then somebody is going to have to draw a line and say enough is enough. Ice sculptures get made every day, but you don't see a whole lot made out of 'molten' ice. Or to put it another way, I've heard it said that completing a project is like walking on water: both are easy if things are frozen.

If, on the other hand, what you want to do hasn't changed, it's just not getting done, you may be facing a basement problem. Some of the signs of a basement problem are seemingly simple changes that have effects on an inordinate amount of other parts of the system;

'bolted on' sections — parts of the solution that don't really fit in with where they are; and clones — partial solutions that have to be repeated in multiple places and that have to be individually maintained. You often see all of these at the same time.

Here's **why** each of these indicates a possible 'add a basement' type change.

Massive ripple effects: If a change winds up touching over half of the system, that's a real good sign that it's something you needed to take into account in the design phase. You can't judge just by the extent of the change though. You could just be going through painting everything blue, or making some other pervasive, but essentially meaningless change that it would have been **better** to make up front, but which won't kill you to do now.

Bolted on baggage: In electronics, you'll often see a small board added on to another board, usually plugged into the socket for a chip and featuring that chip plus other components. Everywhere I worked officially referred to these as daughter boards, but we all called them wart boards. They're used to fix something that would otherwise require a change to the board design. The warts on your project may not be so easy for others to spot, but to the people on the inside they're usually pretty clear. These sorts of changes tend to make the project awkward and unwieldy, with a tendency to fall over a lot. They get in the way of the smooth functioning of other parts of the project, and just generally don't seem to quite belong. That may well be the problem: you may have added something that you shouldn't have – like making a combination power can opener and manure spreader. The combination **can** be made to work, but are you **sure** it's a good idea?

Clones: If there's some part of your solution that requires cloning, you're either making efficient use of available resources, or need to start over. I find the key to figuring out which is which is in how you handle changes. If you're having to make identical changes to each and every clone, it's time to back up. If the parts go in and vanish ("parts is parts"), then you're OK. An example of the good kind is 3/4" steel bolts. If you're using them, you're probably using a lot of them, and you want them all to be the same. But if in one spot you need a longer bolt, you probably aren't going to have to go extend all of the other bolts. On the other hand, if you decide that you need a picture of whoever is at the door, and you built things so you can't use a video camera, you've got a problem that will **not** be fun to solve.

The earlier you can catch these basement changes, the better things will go. If you persevere, the money holds out, and you've got the time, you usually **can** add a basement to your existing building — but would you want to spend a lot of time on the 42nd floor in a strong wind?

These 90% done problems have a nasty tendency to kill projects, one way or another. The good ways are when you kill a project to start over, or bring in someone else to get it working, which often involves **them** starting things over. The bad ways are pretty much what you would expect: project fails, things get shut down, blame gets spread, etc..

One of the saddest cases of this sort of thing I know about is the Superconducting Super Collider, or SSC. The SSC was to be America's, and the world's, premier particle accelerator. With the SSC, we'd be able to push the frontiers of physics back almost to the big bang itself. It wasn't going to be cheap, and it wasn't going to be small – they dug a circular tunnel seven miles in diameter under a big patch of Texas. But as they were getting things going, something terrible happened: a tremendous breakthrough was made in superconductors. You see, the SSC required magnets so powerful that they could only be made by using superconductors. When they did the initial design, all available superconductors required cooling down to liquid hydrogen temperatures – just about as cold as it's possible to get, and definitely not cheap. But just as they were starting work, someone discovered a type of superconductor that worked at liquid **nitrogen** temperatures. Still cold enough to freeze flesh at a touch, but immensely warmer (and **cheaper**) than liquid hydrogen. The problem was, while they now knew that these superconductors **could** be made, they couldn't actually be made **yet**. So; did they build the SSC with working, but hideously expensive liquid hydrogen superconductors, or re-design for how they **thought** the new liquid nitrogen ones would work and hope they'd be ready for use in time (and work like they thought)? With literally **trillions** of dollars at stake, and the US Congress involved, there was a **lot** of confusion and confrontation. To avoid wasting even more money if work were held up and a solution was reached, work continued on building as much as they could. By the time they finally waffled the poor thing to death, they had spent several billion dollars making a nice big underground tube. Last I heard, it was being used to raise mushrooms. Just something to remember if you have a failure you need to compare to something worse so it doesn't seem so bad.

Most projects don't end in quite so much ignominy, or at least don't get as much press when they do. Usually what happens is that you wind up shipping the prototype hoping you'll get a chance to work the bugs out before it hits production, and then wind up watching thousands of the blasted things flow out one door while almost as many come back in through the 'returned as defective' door. Every now and then I run across something that's got a 'feature' so annoying I just **know** I'm looking at something the people involved wish they had a chance to do over.

If you have **any** doubts about a project, try **really** hard to get to do a real prototype. Architects and car designers build scale models. That way they get to see how things will look without having to worry about someone trying to ship it before they get a chance to use what they learned building the model. Some things you can't prototype, in which case you want to put as much effort as possible into the design phase, and in checking your work early and often. Or maybe learning to raise mushrooms.

Chapter 7 — The 80/20 Rule

"If you have no idea how to attack a problem, try solving as many as possible of the problems around it."

I'm sure you've heard of the 80/20 rule in at least one of its many forms. For our purposes, we're interested in the version: "20% of the problems take 80% of the time."

That has a couple of implications for us here. One is that we should focus our efforts on identifying those 20-percenters and figuring out how we're going to solve them. The other is that we should probably try to solve them **first**, since any changes they cause are going to ripple back through how we handle the rest of the problem.

Once we've broken down the problem and found our "terrible 20%," what's the next thing we do? Break that section down! The more we can break things down, the smaller we can make that 'hard to solve' part. If we get lucky, we might even be able to move that hard to do piece off into something someone **else** can do for us. If the hard part of getting to Detroit is covering the actual distance in the time allotted, we might be able to solve that by buying a ticket on a plane. If the distance is over 1,000 miles and the time is 10 minutes, we'll have to do a bit more work.

Just looking at that problem of needing to be at something 1,000 miles away in about 10 minutes you **know** it's too tricky to solve. Rather than giving up, let's see what we **can** solve of this problem.

First, let's see if we're solving the **right** problem. Exactly **why** do we need to be so far away so soon? If it's because we're getting married, we're back to the big problem. If it's just for some sort of a meeting, we've got something we can work with.

Let's assume the following situation: one of your co-workers (let's call him Bob) flew out to make a **big** presentation to a major client. Getting or not getting this job can make or break the company. It's 12:45 and the presentation is scheduled for 1:00. You've just gotten a call from Bob. Bob is on his way over to make the presentation. Problem is, he's in the elevator. Still. Been there for 15 minutes. Building maintenance says it should only be a couple of hours. You and Bob did the whole presentation. No one else can do the job. If you don't make the meeting, you **know** they'll go with your competition. How can you solve this terrible dilemma?

OK, now **this** we might be able to deal with. It's not really that you need to **be** in this other city, but that you need to make a **presentation** there. We still have no idea how we're going to pull this off, but we can start breaking it down and working on the pieces. First, the obvious hard part is that Bob has all of the handouts and such with him. We can tell we won't be able to solve that one from here in time to do any good. We **can** tell Bob to start calling anybody and everybody who might be able to haul him (and those binders) out of that deathtrap: window washers, mountain rescue, Boy Scouts, pretty much anybody with a rope. Basically, we're giving Bob the hard 20%. He's got nothing better to do right now anyway. In the meantime, we'll work on the problem of being at the meeting from two states away.

Let's see, what do we need to do in order to make this presentation? Well, we need to talk to the group, show them some slides and graphs, and get them the handouts.

Taking each of those in order, what are some of the ways we can accomplish the task in the time we have available? And is there any way we can: A) get more time so Bob has a chance to get there; and B) turn this hideous disaster into something that makes us look good?

Talk to the people: Lots of ways we can do this at a distance. Easiest is to just grab a phone and call. We should probably call the secretary of the big boss at the other end and explain the situation. Secretaries are often the ones who have to solve problems, so they might be able to help. For one thing, they can tell you what kind of remote access equipment they have at their end. They can give you phone numbers for speaker phones, fax machines, etc., and they can help you put a good face on the situation. We're in a hurry, so we'll start off with a speaker phone on their end and a cell phone (for mobility) on our end. That covers the basics of making the talk.

Show our slides and graphs: We've actually got several choices here, based on what sort of setups are available at each end. None of them will be quite as good as being there, but if we **could** be there, we wouldn't be doing this. Some of the possible ways we can get our stuff in front of them include emailing copies to that helpful secretary to be printed and/or displayed there, Skype and the other tele-conferencing systems, assuming we can find one we're both on, or can be on in time.

OK, it's just about 1:00 and we actually have things somewhat under control. We're set up to start talking, our slides are being emailed to be passed around, and even if Bob winds up dropping like a rock to his doom, we can overnight the follow-ups to everyone at the meeting because now our secretary has the attendees' names and addresses from the secretary at that end.

We've bought time for Bob to get there and take over for the big finish, and not only that, we've shown that **our** company can get the job done no matter **what** happens. That'll probably score us a point or two over the guy who is there, but didn't bring enough copies of his handouts.

Notice that we never even **tried** to solve the original problem. Unless he walks in the room at the far end, we won't know if Bob made it out of that blasted elevator until everything's over. By solving everything we **could** solve, we made that problem almost not matter.

In other cases, you can solve impossible problems by solving problems that are **close** to the real problem. In math, this is called Successive Approximation. In programming, it's Linear Programming. In both cases, you try for something **close** to solving the real problem, see if the answer looks good enough, then try again in a slightly different way. You keep doing this until you either get a close enough answer or get tired of trying.

The classic example for Linear Programming is called the "Traveling Salesman" problem, where you have to find the most efficient route for a salesman to travel though a list of cities. The actual correct answer to solving this one is to **guess**. Pick a route, any route, and figure out how efficient it is, then pick another route. If it's more efficient, remember it and try again. Keep this up until you get one that's 'good enough.' Actually, there are whole books on different ways to do this, but the simple explanation is good enough for our purposes.

Successive Approximation is the same sort of thing in math. You start with a guess for the answer, and then check it. If it's too high, make your next guess a little lower. If it's too low, guess higher. Once again, there are a lot of complicated things that may be going on here, but that's the thumbnail description.

Going back to our dangling partner problem earlier, you'll notice that we did the same sort of thing in solving it. We came up with an initial try at solving each part, and kept working at it until we either got through with that part or found something better. That's the reason we went with a cell phone instead of a land line. Because we could move around, we were able to get over to our fancy video conference room. When we got there, we switched from just being on speaker to being 'almost' in the room. Sure, they had to look at emailed copies of the charts we put up on the screen, but at least we sounded better and they had something other than a speaker phone to look at.

So our summary from this chapter is:

"If you have no idea how to attack a problem, try solving as many as possible of the problems around it."

Most of the parts of a problem are easy. The ones that aren't are the ones we'd **like** to solve first. If we can't find a way to break them down into chunks we can handle, we want to at least be making **some** progress on the problem.

If you can solve enough of the little problems, you might be able to make the big ones go away, or at least get smaller.

If you can't find an answer, guess. If you guess wrong (and you probably will or you wouldn't be guessing), try to figure out what's wrong with your guess and make a new, adjusted guess. Even if you never quite solve the problem, at least you'll get closer, and if you get close enough, it won't matter. The old adage "close only counts in horseshoes and hand grenades" really points out that a hand grenade is a simplified solution to throwing a rock accurately enough to bring down a foe.

Chapter 8 — Ideal Gasses

One of the 'extra' principles I simplified out of my list is:

"If a problem looks too complex, look for ways to break it down into manageable chunks."

It's not a bad principle, it's just that it's pretty well overlapped by my second and sixth principles, and I didn't want to be telling people to memorize a long, complex list of ways to simplify things.

There are some subtle differences between what this one covers and the other two though, which is why I based this chapter on it. While my second principle tells us:
"It's easier to solve a lot of small, simple, problems than one big complex one"
and the sixth principle advises:
"If you have no idea how to attack a problem, try solving as many of the problems 'around' it as you can."
this one targets just how you want to go about turning your messy problem into a set of simple problems.

It's not just a matter of pulling off random bits and hoping that will make things easier. Flailing blindly usually just makes things harder. You have to look for the seams in things, find ways to break them down into the known and the unknown.

Sometimes you'll wind up with a subset of the problem where most of the individual pieces are solvable, but the combination is just too much. Fortunately, there's a long-standing precedent for what to do in these cases: solve a simpler version and just assume that the simple answer scales up.

Actually, you may need to do it a bit more carefully than that. I'd recommend that you look at this as part of the Successive Approximation technique I talked about in Chapter 7. Make some simplifying assumptions, solve the problem using them, then check your work. If the answer isn't close enough, change some of your simplifications and try again.

The bad part of this can be the time and effort involved — sometimes it's more work to come up with a good set of simplifications than it would be to slog through the original problem. **But** if you're ever going to have to solve this same sort of problem **again**, you've got a good chance of coming out ahead. In fact, having a reliable way to find a quick and close answer to something can be one of those niche markets I mentioned back in Chapter 3.

The title for this chapter comes from just such a simplified version of a complex problem. In Physics, they quickly realized that calculating what was actually going on in most situations was far too complex. Even now, when we have computers to do the grunt work at incredible speeds, there's just not enough time to solve these things in detail. So the Physics people came up with the concept of Ideal Gasses — gasses in which all of the fine details didn't matter and could be ignored. This let them solve the problems they were working on, even if they did have to work out fudge factors for real world conditions.

Most of Physics started in these simplified worlds, and they're still used in teaching today. Over the centuries these models have been polished and refined. More and more of the differences between the Ideal and Real World versions have been quantified and/or reduced. New ways of attacking some of the problems have been found, and new tools, such as computers, have made it possible to crunch through problems that couldn't have been solved before.

But in the end, the simplified model still rules. The latest and hottest simulations of airflow over an airplane wing, for example, only look at scattered points along the wing, not each and every point. I think they can handle a sub-1 centimeter grid, at least for some wings, but to be completely accurate, they'd have to tighten that up until they accounted for every molecule. When you look at it in one way, the points they model are such a small fraction of the total number of points they **could** model that they're essentially ignoring the whole wing.

Of course, the **reason** they can get away with this sort of thing is that the details don't matter, or at least they don't matter all that much. When the Wright brothers designed their plane, it was large and slow enough that they could basically eyeball the whole thing. The supersonic Stealth fighter is so close to the edge of what can be done it can only be flown by a computer that tries to see what's actually happening and figure out what tiny changes to make to get what the pilot wants done to happen. I'm sure the pilots are happy that it does the job so well, but if we could get an even more detailed model of the airflow, we could make it do it even better.

Since very few of us will have to worry about designing supersonic fighter jets, how about a more common example?

When I bought my house, **everyone** had a complicated set of formulas to figure out how much house we could afford. After having gone through three or four of these things, I came up with my own system, one that the people I mention it to say still works, albeit roughly.

My formula for how much house you can afford to buy: Double your income. That's it. It's not **exactly** right, but it will get you close enough to know if you're wasting your time or not.

If you, or someone you know, is looking to buy a house, try this test. Have them start looking at houses using my formula, then, when they find one they're interested in that comes close enough to what I say, run through the realtor's system. Then the lender's system. Then, if they actually buy the place, could they **really** afford it? Hopefully what you'll see is that, if the house met my criteria, it also met everyone else's – including the all-important real world test.

So, now that we've decided to give this 'Ideal Gasses' thing a try, how do we go about doing it? Personally, I start by backing up. The farther away something is, the fewer details you can see. I know, I know – another stunning revelation. Remember, this **is** a book on making things simple.

Let's go back to those Ideal Gas laws for a moment. The reason they exist is because it's too difficult to deal with the details of the flow of a gas. By backing up and away from the troubling molecule by molecule view, we're able to get a pretty accurate picture of a gust of wind. In a similar vein, while you may not be able to predict what any **one** customer will want to buy, you have a pretty good idea of what **most** people want and can put it right up front. We're ignoring the details to get a pattern.

Another way to get the pattern is to ask somebody who knows. That's effectively what I did for my 'affordability' system. By the time I'd been through a couple of the more complex systems, I was able to find a rough correlation between their result and my income.

Take a look at your problem. By now you should have broken it down at least once, possibly many times. Now we want to take the descriptions of those chunks and put them back together again. Usually not the whole thing, at least not at once. Start with the two most closely related parts and try to come up with a simple description of the combined problem. Then do a couple of others, etc., until you've backed up one whole layer. If it's still too complex, back out again. Eventually you should either find something you can take a stab at, or get back to a restated version of the original problem.

If you **do** get all the way back out without finding an answer, try moving out one or two levels **more**. Can't hurt. Might help. Let's say your problem is that your key broke off in the front door and you can't get in the house. When you back away from that, it becomes "The front door is locked and I can't unlock it." Maybe you don't have to. Is there another way in? If not, back up again to: "I can't get in my house." Once again, why do you need to get in? Perhaps you can just go to a neighbor's house. If you can, then you can use their phone to call someone to come fix your door.

I've been telling you over and over to take a closer look at your problem, to break it down into smaller and smaller parts, but sometimes the right answer can only be found by stepping back. The problem you can't solve in one context may be easy to solve in another. It may even turn out to be one you don't have to solve at all. If your car leaks oil, and you can't seem to get it fixed, you might not care if you're going to be getting a new car anyway. And even if you **do** still care, knowing that you're getting a new car lets you find another way to look at the problem. It's no longer "my car is leaking oil" but something like "I need to keep this car running two more weeks." That one you can probably solve by just buying some more oil and adding it as needed. The leak itself might be almost impossible to fix.

So when you're faced with a complex problem, and you're looking for ways to break it down, look for what you can simplify. Even if you have to go back and 'fill in the blanks' later, it gives you a place to start. And don't forget to step back every now and then, just in case that thing blocking your view of the forest turns out to be a tree.

Chapter 9 — Calling For Help

Sooner or later you're going to run into a problem you just can't, or don't want to, solve. Often it's a problem that you **could** solve, if you wanted to spend the time and money.

Back in Chapter 5 I mentioned that I do very few home repairs or improvements myself. It's not because I **can't** do most things, it's just that by the time I screw up and hurt myself it would have been cheaper to have called in a professional in the beginning. Eventually, I started to figure this out, and by now I have a fairly good idea of when it's more cost-effective to pay for something up front.

In the same way, you need to learn where and when you should call for help in solving problems. You don't need some high-powered team for every little thing that comes up, but you're probably going to at least **talk** to someone in many situations.

Let's look at some of the reasons you might want to call in an expert to help with your problem:

1) "It's not my job." – Probably the most common reason for calling in someone else is that the project calls for skills outside your area of expertise. I've never

met anyone who really was an expert in everything, and even the few folks I know who are good at most things still call in pros when they're needed. I've mentioned before that even though I've been programming for over 30 years **I** stay out of some things. I probably **could** do them, but it would take me a lot longer to do a decent job.

2) Do you have what it takes? – I don't do much work on my own car. Partly that's **because** I don't do much work on my own car (meaning I don't have a lot of expertise). There's also the fact that working on a modern vehicle can require a lot of special tools I don't own. I could buy most of them, but why? Some of those tools are so expensive that I'd have to have my car break down so many times I'd be more likely to dump it off a cliff than of ever make owning that tool cost effective.

3) Have you got the time? – Suppose I decide I **do** want to work on my car, and I've found a toolbox under a rock somewhere. It's still going to take me a lot longer to do it than it would a regular mechanic, because I've got to take the time to learn how. If I don't care that it will take me eight hours to do something he could do in 20 minutes, there's still a potential problem: what **else** should I have been doing in those seven-plus hours I just wasted?

4) What if you're wrong? – Keeping with our car repair theme, some things have very minor consequences. If I

don't do a good job on replacing the bulb in my dome light, no big deal. Same thing for the fuse for the radio. Annoying, but not critical. But there's a whole list of things I wouldn't want failing at highway speeds in rush hour traffic. Let's see, brakes, steering, transmission, how about having a wheel come off? If it's **got** to be right, make sure you trust whoever does the work, be it yourself or someone you hire.

5) That's disgusting! – If my sink is running slow, I'll take a look at it. A couple of times in winters the shower drain has frozen and made the shower back up. I fixed it myself. If the toilet starts backing up into the sink, I'm calling in a pro and standing well back (and upwind). Sometimes we run into things we just would rather not have to deal with. This is the sign of a pretty lucrative niche market, by the way. If you don't mind doing something people hate to do, your rate will basically be set by how much they hate it and how much competition you have. CPA's at tax time are a good example of this.

With all of that in mind, sometimes you **won't** call in help. Let's go back over that same list and look at why you might want to tough it out and do it yourself.

1) "It's not my job." – Well, how **else** do you expect to learn anything new? If you **always** call in someone else, you'd better hope there's a lifetime demand for whatever it is you do, and that you'll never be stranded someplace. As I said, I don't generally work on my car, but I **do**

know enough to (usually) get it back on the road long enough to get to a garage.

2) Do you have what it takes? – Many specialty tools can be rented, others can be acquired used. The corollary for the kind of tools I usually use – software – is older versions. They're often available for reduced prices from either the original vendor or surplus houses. I do have to confess though, that sometimes I do things myself just as an excuse to get the required tools – one of the hazards of being a gadget freak.

3) Have you got the time? – If you've got other things you should be doing, you probably should get them done. But sometimes you **can't** do anything else until this gets done, and you can't wait for anyone else. Sometimes that cost/benefit ratio **demands** that you do the work yourself. If an expert costs $200/hour and can do the job in two hours, that gives you 40 hours to get it right if your time's only worth $10/hour. I've worked with people that spent hundreds of hours restoring old cars. Not very cost effective, until you consider the fact that they **liked** restoring old cars. If it's your hobby, the time hardly matters.

4) What if you're wrong? – Sometimes, this is the most important reason to do it yourself. If I'm at all capable of doing a critical job, I'm going to at least do my best to check the work of whoever does the task. Anytime there's a risk of serious harm to my precious pink skin, I take a great interest in quality control.

5) That's disgusting! – This is a relative item. If you've got no sense of smell, pumping septic tanks probably won't bother you that much. Sometimes something's bad enough that you really don't have any choice but to do it yourself. Sometimes you have things you'd rather not have known. Not to be macabre, but how many murderers call in someone else to dispose of the body? Actually, that's of those niche markets I mentioned: cleaning up after the deceased. They're usually called in after a violent death, or one that wasn't found right away. (Sorry if you were reading this over lunch.)

So now that we've looked at some of the reasons for and against calling in a pro, what else can we say about the subject?

Well, sometimes you call in a pro as a learning aid. I don't mean specifically as an instructor, more like an example. I've mentioned before that I go to a professional whenever my tax situation changes. In between, I do them myself, but if I'm unsure about anything, I figure it's cheaper to pay an accountant up front than an auditor down the line.

If you're calling in a pro as a learning aid you want to make sure to discuss this with them up front. Some people don't like being watched. Some might charge a little extra to go slow and explain what they're doing. Others may be flattered that you think they're so good you want to use them as a model. Often they'll adjust what they do and how they do it to help you learn. There are professionals in almost every line that specialize in sharing their knowledge. Going back to my car repair example, think of all of the people who host the various television and radio shows.

One important thing to remember about hiring professionals: if you're good at your job, you're probably going to make it look easy. Don't feel cheated if you thought something was going to be a major problem and the person you called in just stares at it for a while, then does fifteen minutes of work. Those hours spent studying the problem are probably **why** they could do the work so quickly. Plus, you're probably paying for their having some specialty tool. The guy at the quick lube can change my oil in ten minutes, which is a **lot** faster than I can, but then again, I don't have a pit or a rack in my garage.

When you hire an expert, you're paying for their expertise. There's the old joke about the fellow who ran an isolated town's power station for years and years. It was a fairly easy task, because the station was almost totally automated, but since he was out in the middle of nowhere, it was also pretty lonely. Well, after thirty years he decided to retire, and the town found two bright young lads to come take over from him. He trained them well, and then moved into town and settled down to enjoy his rest. Things went smoothly for six months or so, then the power went out. After three days, the townspeople came to the old man and asked for his help.

He was very reluctant, but after they promised him $50,000, he agreed to go on out. When he arrived, the haggard looking young lads explained what they had done, showed him reams of test results, walked him through the areas they had worked on, etc. After all of this, the old man went to the control panel and pressed the START button. There was a whirr, a clunk, and then nothing. He picked up a hammer and stepping over to a panel, hit it three solid whacks. This time when he pressed the START button, everything went fine. The townsfolk were ecstatic and cried out how happy they were he'd been able to fix it for free. The old man stolidly demanded his $50,000. "But all you did was hit it three times with a hammer!" they cried, "Surely you're not charging us $50,000 for **that!**" "No," he replied. "Hitting it with the hammer is only costing you $100. I'm also charging $900 for taking the time to come all the way out here and go through the whole plant. The other $49,000 is for the thirty years it took to know **where** to hit it."

Hindsight is generally 20/20, but it's not often cheap to get the experience to recognize a problem when you see it again.

So to sum things up, when you're working on a problem watch for those areas where you may need or want the help of a professional. If you think you might need a pro's help, look at the cost/benefit ratio of having it done versus doing it yourself. If you're going to have to do this same sort of thing again, you might consider having a pro teach you how to do it yourself next time. If you do hire a pro, be prepared for them making it look easy – that's **why** they're professionals. Time spent studying a problem is only time wasted if you already know exactly what to do.

Chapter 10 — The Real World

We've gone through a lot of ways to simplify and ultimately solve your problems. We've talked about how to break your problem down into manageable chunks, and about how to arrange those chunks so you can get someone else to solve that part for you. We've looked at making sure we weren't wasting time and money solving the wrong problem, and we've touched on why you might, or might not, want to call in outside help. This chapter will wrap it all up with a look at some real world uses of these techniques.

Let's start off by reviewing the Three Principles of Problem Simplification:

1) Before you try to solve a problem, make sure you know what the problem really is.

2) It's easier to solve a lot of small, simple, problems than one big complex problem.

3) Every problem has a clear and simple answer. It's wrong, but figuring out why it's wrong will usually lead you to the right answer.

And once again, the mnemomic to help you remember the principles is **PIE**.

P – Pieces. Cut your problem up into easier to solve pieces just like you would cut up a pie.
I – Identify. Before you try to solve your problem, make sure you know what the problem really is.
E – Easy Answer. Yes, that simple answer is probably wrong, but it will help you find the real one.

And, just to save you some flipping through the book, here are the 'other' principles — the ones I simplified off of my original list for various reasons, but wanted to include in this discussion.

"Sometimes it's cheaper to spend money on simplifying a problem than it is to solve the complex version."

"The energy required to change course increases geometrically with time, so make sure you know where you're going before you leave."

"If you have no idea how to attack a problem, try solving as many of the problems 'around' it as you can."

"If a problem looks too complex, look for ways to break it down into manageable chunks."

If you're a stickler for seven-step systems, feel free to put all of them on a list. If you want something simple, stick with the big three and just try to keep the general ideas of the others in mind.

Now how about some of those real world examples of Problem Simplification.

We'll start with a real simple one, a problem everybody runs into and which somehow makes itself a much bigger problem than it should be: Tipping. Not as in cows, but as in gratuities for your server. I assume you can decide for yourself what percentage you want — the 'standard' 15% or some other value — but it's amazing how hard it can be to figure out what 15% comes out to. Do what I do: break it down and solve a simpler version. Assume the bill was $27.50 and we want to leave 15%. First, figure out 10%. That's dead easy — all you do is move the decimal point and maybe round a bit. So we've got 10% as $2.75 — how does that give us our desired 15%? Well, what's half of 10? Obviously 5, so if we take half of that 10% tip ($2.75), we'll have 5% ($1.38) and we can add them together to get 15% ($4.13). If you think they did a little bit better or worse, take that easy to get 10% and use it to get 1%. You can go straight off the original number if you want to be daring. In this case 1% is 28 cents. Personally, I usually adjust the tip up or down to a 'convenient' number, so I'd leave either $4.25 or an even $4, depending on how the service was. Actually, I'd probably just drop $32.00 on the tray and walk off. That makes the tip $4.50, which is only about 16% ($4.13 + $0.28 = $4.41).

83

In figuring the tip, I'll probably make use of another real world application of Problem Simplification — arithmetic. I actually learned this trick back in my high school Geometry class. Break the problem down into easy to solve pieces and then combine them for the answer. As an example of another percentage problem, what's $38.00 after a 10% discount? I do it by saying, "10% of $38 is $3.80, or 20 cents less than $4, so 10% off of $38 is $34 ($38 - $4) plus 20 cents difference for a result of $34.20."

To find 13 * 27, I'll usually do something along the lines of 10 * 27 = 270 + 3 * 25 = 75 = 345 + 3 * 2 = 6 = 351. Going a bit slower to explain the steps, I break the 13 down into a 10 and a 3. 10 times anything is easy, so I get 10 * 27 or 270. 3 * 27 looks hard, but I already know 3 * 25, so I add that part (75) and that leaves me with an easy 3 * 2.

Other times I'll do it slightly differently. Say instead of 13 * 27 it's 19 * 23. The simple way for me to solve this is 20 * 23 = 460; 460 - 23 = 440 - 3 = 437. Notice that this time I went **up** to an easy answer, and in subtracting back down to the real result, I once again went with the simple steps. I could go on, but I've found that this either makes sense or it doesn't, apparently based on how you learned to do arithmetic. If it seems like it **might** make sense, try it when you can and it will probably wind up working for you. If it's not making any sense at all for you, don't worry about it. Using these techniques would make math more complicated, rather than simpler, for you. Most people I've met who can't use these methods have 'simpler' methods of their own that make no apparent sense to me.

That's another important point: what's simpler for one person may not be simpler for another person. Try the things that have worked for others (that is, of course, the simple way to find a shortcut), but if they don't work for you, keep looking for your own simpler way to do things. At worst, someone else's shortcut will either guide you towards yours, or tell you what to stay away from.

If you look around, you'll find that you're already using any number of real world Problem Simplifications. We set them up all the time. If there's a tedious, or complicated task out there, there's a simplification to try and deal with it. Usually more than one.

Want some examples? Here you go:

The interstate highway system: The interstates were designed to simplify moving around the country, especially moving military equipment. That's why no interstates exceed certain grades on hills, and what determined the minimum load limits for bridges.

The telephone: Generally a lot simpler than running down the street to talk to someone else.

The pager: Intended to be simpler than calling around to

find someone, or having them call in every time they move from one place to another.

The cell phone: now you have the ease of reaching out to someone the pager gave, while still being able to talk to them wherever they are. And of course, these days most people send a text rather than make a call.

Ball point pens: If you've ever used a pen that **doesn't** have its own nice, neat, built-in ink supply, you should appreciate how much simpler a ball point makes writing.

Mechanical pencils: **Much** easier to sharpen than a wooden pencil. So easy, in fact, that you never have to do it (which is about as simple as it gets).

I could go on for several pages, but I think it's simpler just to let you find your own examples.

Although I **do** have just one more example of real world Problem Simplification I want to bring up, since it's so very relevant to this book.

Writing a book is a fairly complex and tedious task. If I'd tried to just start writing until I had enough stuff for a book, I probably wouldn't have ever finished. There's a good chance I wouldn't even have been able to get started on such a daunting task. But fortunately, someone else long ago came up with the idea of writing an outline when doing a long document. The outline let me break the problem of writing this book down into manageable chunks. First I roughly laid out what was going to be in the book, then I fiddled about with it until I was fairly happy with the way I had the major portions arranged.

After that, I went into each major section, or chapter, and outlined what I was going to say in it. Some chapters got fairly detailed outlines, and others got just a couple of notes — whatever I felt I needed to do the job right.

When I had the full outline, I went through it and made a few more changes, moving some things around, combining a couple of prospective chapters, splitting up others, that sort of thing. Since the whole outline is only about two pages long, it wasn't that hard. With the whole book weighing in around 20,000 words, it would have been tough to do these sort of changes at the end.

So, to summarize this chapter, and the book as a whole, all I can really say is: if it looks too complicated, it probably is. Rather than fighting with some great, unruly mass, look for a way to simplify the problem. You can waste a lot more time by traveling at a good clip in the wrong direction than you'll spend planning the trip.

I hope you've found this book helpful, and that what you've learned will continue to help you down the road. As for me, I'll take the simple way out here and say…

The end.

About the Author

Steven L. Van Dyke is often described as an oddly useful person, even if he does have to do it himself. A somewhat retired (not by choice) Software Engineer, he lives in Kansas City with his ever-indulgent wife, 3 cats, and a surprising number of ways to roast and brew coffee.

While he no longer juggles professionally he may be available to help you find the simple solution to your complex problem. You can ask him at problems@svandyke.com

I don't have any other books to plug here but Dr. Hans G. Schantz, who helped me get this book actually published has some really good ones. Check him out on Amazon.

One Last Thing:

If you enjoyed this book and/or found it useful it would really help me out if you would leave at least a short review on Amazon. Your support really does make a difference and like many authors I read every review.

www.ingramcontent.com/pod-product-compliance
Lightning Source LLC
Chambersburg PA
CBHW031924170526
45157CB00008B/3042